SMALL GRACES

*The Quiet Gifts
of
Everyday Life*

By the Author

Simple Truths
Letters to My Son
Haunting Reverence
Neither Wolf nor Dog

Edited by the Author

Native American Wisdom
The Soul of an Indian
The Wisdom of the Great Chiefs

SMALL GRACES

*The Quiet Gifts
of
Everyday Life*

KENT NERBURN

NEW WORLD LIBRARY

NOVATO, CALIFORNIA

New World Library
14 Pamaron Way
Novato, California

© 1998 Kent Nerburn

Cover design: Michele Wetherbee
Cover photograph: Leigh Beisch
Text design: Aaron Kenedi

Two of the pieces herein appeared in
substantially similar form in the author's
earlier work *Letters to My Son*.

Library of Congress Cataloging-in-Publication Data
Nerburn, Kent, 1946–
Small graces : the quiet gifts of everyday life / Kent Nerburn.
p.   cm.
ISBN 1-57731-072-1 (hardcover : alk. paper)
1. Spiritual life.   I. Title
BL624.N46   1998   98-5115
291.4'32—dc21   CIP

ISBN 1-57731-072-1
First printing, April 1998
Printed in the U.S.A. on acid-free paper
Distributed to the trade by Publishers Group West

10 9 8 7 6 5 4 3 2

*The true joy of life is not in
the grand gesture but in the
consecration of the moment.*

CONTENTS

Gatherings

Departures

INTRODUCTION

We dream our lives in grand gestures, but we live our lives in small moments. From our first rising at the dawn, to our last conscious thoughts at night, our lives are spent in tasks that absorb our attention and keep us from contemplating the great issues that lie at the heart of life.

Why are we here? What is love? Does God exist? What lies behind the veil of death?

These are the questions that make us human. But their answers, and even their contemplation, seem far beyond the ordinary realms in which we live our days.

We want to live spiritual lives. We know, at heart, that we are spiritual beings. But our lives are small, our concerns immediate. The days we live seem to conspire against our spiritual selves. We look longingly at those who shine great light into this world — Mother Teresa, Gandhi, Martin Luther King — and our lives and accomplishments seem paltry in comparison.

We dream of the touch on our shoulder that will call us to greatness, to an act that would change the world. But the touches on our shoulder call us only to the small acts of everyday life — changing diapers, changing lightbulbs, changing schedules. Far from being exalted beings, we seem to be prisoners of the ordinary, and we are haunted by the insignificance of our days.

We must learn to see with other eyes. The world contains many paths, some exalted, some mundane. It is not our task to judge the worthiness of our path; it is our task to walk our path with worthiness. We have been blinded by the bright light of heroes and saints. We must learn to trust the small light we are given, and to value the light that we can shed into the lives of those around us.

We must never forget that the mindful practice of daily affairs is also a path into the realm of the spirit. The Japanese have long known this, and hallowed the ordinary moments of life by elevating them into art. The Native Americans have also understood this, and consecrated everyday actions by surrounding them with ceremony and prayer.

But ours is a transient life, lived on the run, with an endless sense of process, of movement, of chasing the future. We seldom pause to shine a light upon the ordinary moments, to hallow them with our own attentiveness, to honor them with gentle caring. They pass unnoticed, lost in the ongoing rush of time.

Yet it is just such a hallowing that our lives require. We need to find ways to lift the moments of our daily lives — to celebrate and consecrate the ordinary, to allow the light of spiritual awareness to illuminate our days.

For though we may not live a holy life, we live in a world alive with holy moments. We need only take the time to bring these moments into the light.

AN OFFERING
TO A QUIET GOD

*We see no need for the setting apart
one day in seven as holy, for to us all
days belong to God.*

— Ohiyesa, Dakotah Sioux

There are those who search for God in the quiet places — no churches, no public displays of piety, no dramatic or flamboyant rituals.

They may be found standing in humble awe before a sunset, or weeping quietly at the beauty of a Bach concerto, or filled with an overflowing of pure love at the sight of an infant in the arms of its mother.

You may meet them visiting the elderly, comforting the lonely, feeding the hungry, and caring for the sick.

The greatest among them may give away what they own in the name of compassion and goodness, while never once uttering the word "God" out loud. Or they may do no more than offer a smile or a hand to someone in need, or quietly bow their heads at a moment of beauty that passes through their lives, and say a simple prayer of gratitude to the spirit that has created us all.

They are the lovers of the quiet God, the believers in the small graces of ordinary life.

Theirs is not the grand way, the way of the mystic or the preacher or the zealot or the saint. Some would say that theirs is not a way at all. All they know for certain is that life has a beauty and a joy that transcends all the darkness that surrounds us, that something ineffable lives beyond the ordinary affairs of the day, and that without this mystery our lives would not be worth living.

This book is dedicated to those who search for the quiet God, who seek the spirit in the small moments of our everyday life. It is a celebration of the ordinary, a reminder that when all else is stripped away, a life lived with love is enough.

awakenings

Morning is the dream renewed, the heart refreshed, earth's forgiveness painted in the colors of the dawn.

THE GIFT OF THE DAWN

Each soul must meet the morning
sun, the new sweet earth, and the
Great Silence alone.

— Ohiyesa, Dakotah Sioux

I have risen early today. Far in the distance, a faint glow paints the horizon. Dawn is coming, gently and full of prayer.

I step quietly from my bed, alive to the silences around me. This is the quiet time, the time of innocence and soft thoughts, the childhood of the day.

Now is the moment when I must pause and lift my heart — now, before the day fragments and my consciousness shatters into a thousand pieces. For this is the moment when the senses are most alive, when a thought, a touch, a piece of music can shape the spirit and color the day.

But if I am not careful — if I rise, frantic, from my bed, full of small concerns — the mystical flow of the imagination at rest will be broken, the past and the future will rush in to claim my mind, and I will be swept up into life's petty details and myriad obligations. Gone will be the openness that comes only to the waking heart, and with it, the chance to focus the spirit and consecrate the day.

All the great spiritual traditions have known this. The Christian monastics remain silent until their first chant of morning praise. Muslims begin their day with petitions of humility and thanks. The Dakotah Indians learned as children to walk in silence to a lake or stream, splash water on their faces, then offer up a prayer toward the sun.

Our lives may not allow such exalted devotions. But something precious is lost if we rush headlong into the details of life without pausing for a moment to pay homage to the mystery of life and the gift of another day.

It need not be much. A prayer whispered quietly, a gentle touching of a plant or flower, a momentary gaze upon a sleeping child, a second's stillness in the presence of the light. Any of these will do. What is needed is only a pausing of the heart so the spirit can take wing and be lifted toward the infinite.

I walk silently toward the window. The darkness is lifting. A thin shaft of lavender has creased the horizon, setting the edges of the trees on fire with morning light. I pause and bow my head. For this brief moment, I am held in the hand of God, and I am sent forth into the morning with the poetry of possibility beating in my heart.

We hear the rain, but not the snow. A day well lived must know the shape of silence.

THE ELOQUENCE
OF SILENCE

The silence of creation speaks louder
than the tongues of men or angels.
— Thomas Merton

The silence is profound this morning. It is not portentous; there seems to be nothing in the waiting. It is a gentle silence, liquid and pastel, a shimmer on still waters.

It is good to listen to the silence that surrounds each day. In the same way that music is made alive by the silence that surrounds the notes, a day comes alive by the silence that surrounds our actions. And the dawn is the time when silence reveals herself most clearly.

I once met a man who was raised on the Canadian prairies. We got to talking about the open space, and how it had shaped his spirit. "When the wind stops," he said, "it is so loud that everyone pauses to listen."

The thought intrigued me. How could the end of a sound be loud?

But when I traveled to those prairies, I began to understand. For the people in the great prairies, the sound they hear, the music that underlies their lives, is the constant and ever-present howl of the wind. To them it is no sound at all. When it is removed, the silence takes a different shape, and all are aware of it; all pause to hear.

We need to pay heed to the many silences in our lives. An empty room is alive with a different silence than a room where someone is hiding. The silence of a happy house echoes less darkly than the silence of a house of brooding anger.

The silence of a winter morning is sharper than the silence of a summer dawn. The silence of a mountain pass is larger than the silence of a forest glen.

These are not fantasies, they are subtle discriminations of the senses. Though all are the absence of sound, each silence has a character of its own.

No meditation better clears the mind than to listen to the shape of the silence that surrounds us. It focuses us on the thin line between what is there and what is not there. It opens our heart to the unseen, and reminds us that the world is larger than the events that fill our days.

Into this morning's silence comes the first call of a bird. I listen carefully. It cuts through the silence like a rainbow through the dawn.

Our home is the caretaker of our memories. From our windows, our imaginations take wing.

THE WINDOW
ON THE HEART

I walk to my window to greet the day. I chose this window for my own long ago, as one chooses a chair or a spoon or a mug. I seek it out each morning before the others in the house awake. It faces slightly to the north, so the morning sun enters it obliquely, giving the light the delicious subtlety of indirection. From it I can watch all of life turn toward the coming of the day.

Whenever I have had to move from a house, the memory I have carried with me — the memory that has most animated my spirit — is always the memory of the light, and the way it cascaded in through the windows and illuminated the passing moments of the day.

Sometimes a shaft, sometimes a soft glow, sometimes a brilliant illumination that made me fear that the house itself was on fire. But it is always in the memory of light that the spirit of the house comes to life.

This house I live in now will forever touch my spirit for the way it offers me the dawn. From my window the day arrives like the distant chanting of a prayer.

I sit before the window and watch the growing dawn. A memory of Alice rises before me, for it was Alice who taught me about windows. She was small, frail, framed in a halo of light from the window before which she sat. I approached cautiously, and knelt beside her.

"Alice?" I asked.

She turned to me. Her eyes were cloudy, but filled with light.

"They said you would be willing to talk to me about life here."

She nodded.

This was not a task I had relished. I was writing a small piece about life in nursing homes, and my sense of rage at the heartless way our elders must end their lives had almost overwhelmed me.

My heart had been torn a thousand ways as I had walked the halls and spoken to the residents in these places that claim to care for our aged and give dignity to their final days. It had been a gauntlet of pain and sorrow. The lonely; the incoherent lost in their private memories; the dazed; the angry; those who grabbed your arm and begged, "Daddy, Daddy, take me out of here, I want to go home" — all of them and more had confronted me and filled me with a deep and unassuageable grief.

With each footstep tears welled up within me and I raged against a heartless God, a heartless society, the cruel ways of nature and the sadnesses of life. My heart did not have enough tears to purge the rage and pain that were washing across me.

"You must talk to Alice," the nurses had said. "She will show you something."

Reluctantly I had agreed to do so.

And now I was beside her. She said "Good

morning," but her eyes were staring out the window. I did not wish to disturb her; I kept my silence.

"Look," she said finally, pointing out the window. The traffic flowed noisily below. The cacophony of a life she would never again share rose up from the streets. I stared through her one opening into the outside world. Far in the distance was the cupola of a cathedral.

"Isn't it beautiful?" she said. "I come here every day to watch the sun rise. I've been all over Europe. I've seen Notre Dame and St. Peter's and the Duomo in Florence. But none was more beautiful than this, and I can see it every day."

I looked out. The sun was bursting around the edges of the dome, enveloping it in a halo of pastel light. The sun reflected off her glasses, and I could see the tears in her eyes.

We spoke a bit. I took some notes. But none of that mattered. It was the cathedral, and the dawn, and the radiant morning light that we were sharing. She reached over and grabbed my hand.

"Isn't this a gift?" she said.

I did not know what to say. I had come that morning, prepared to look with sadness on the shrinking horizons of her life, to weep for her lost dreams and the tiny window that framed the boundaries of her day. But those were my tears, not hers. Her tears were for the beauty. From her window she received the spirit of the dawn.

I think often of Alice. She was an artist of the ordinary. The great French Impressionist painter Claude Monet had sat before a window, painting the cathedral at Rouen as the light played upon its surface over the course of a day. Alice was doing no different, but she painted with the colors of her heart.

I left that day changed in some fundamental way. I had wanted to define the walls of Alice's prison; she had wanted to give me the gift of the day. I had wanted to see limitation; she had wanted to show me possibility.

She had taken a moment from the seamless flow of time and space and held it up in private consecration, and we had partaken of it together in a small communion of our spirits.

As I walked back down the hall, one of the nurses who had directed me to Alice looked up from her desk.

"Did she show you something?" she asked.

"Yes," I answered softly.

"Her window?"

"Yes."

"I thought so," she smiled, and went back to work.

I walked out into the morning with the eyes of a child.

Ritual is routine infused with mindfulness. It is habit made holy.

OF COFFEE MUGS
AND MONKS

I take my morning mug of coffee in both hands and lift it ever so slightly toward the sky.

I am alone; there is no one to see.

This is my private gesture — my acknowledgment, my offering, my moment of thankfulness for the gift of this awakening day.

I recall the words of Rikyu, the Zen poet:

> *In my hands, a bowl of tea.*
> *All of nature is revealed in its green color.*
> *Closing my eyes I find green mountains and pure*
> *water within my own heart.*

Silently drinking, I feel these become a part of me.

Perhaps my morning cup of coffee is not so profound. But with this first taste, the fire of life comes alive in me. I sense the richness of the earth, the calming flow of water, the transformative power of fire, the aroma of life and nourishment. All my senses are alert, and my day goes from silence into song.

I think of my Ojibwe friends who see tobacco as a sacrament. To me it is little more than a devastating habit. But in the hands of those who still practice the traditional ways, it is an homage to the Creator.

As one elder told me. "Tobacco comes from the earth. It goes upward toward God. When it has done its work it returns to the earth. When I smoke I am reminded of where we come from and where we must go. It turns my heart toward the Great Mystery."

My morning cup of coffee, though not buoyed by the power of tradition, is not so different. In itself, it is nothing. But partaken with mindfulness, it is a small act of worship, an act of consecration, a prayer of thankfulness to the awakening day.

I am reminded of something I learned while living in a monastery in the mountains of British

Columbia. I had gone there to create a sculpture for the monks, and in order to invest the work with a spiritual presence that would resonate with their hearts I had chosen to live by the rules and dictates of their lives.

The abbot in charge of the monastery was a harsh man, disinclined toward compassion and the human touch. He watched me struggle with the austere rigor of monastic life and the constraints within which the monks conducted their daily affairs.

One day he came over to me and said, with no explanation, "Stay in the machine. It will clean you out."

At first I did not know what he meant. The comment was so flip, so casual, and so out of character, that I almost thought he was teasing or chiding me. But day by day I began to understand.

I rose with the monks, chanted with them, worked when they worked, prayed when they prayed. Gradually, the simple rituals of their daily life, the gentle repetition with which they lived their days, began to focus my being and fill me with peace.

By the time I had finished the sculpture six months later, my spirit had deepened, my heart had cleared, my eyes had opened. I was by no means a monk, but I was a believer in the power of their ways. By following their appointed rituals, I had become a deeper and wiser person. I had stayed in the machine. It had begun to clean me out.

Most of us do not live a life of monastic rigor. Our days are full of jagged edges and jangling moments. But most of us do have quiet routines that inform our lives.

We rise each morning and greet our day in the same fashion. A first cup of coffee, a glance at the paper, a certain way we bathe and prepare for our entry into the day — these do not change. They are the rituals by which we shape our days.

But we do not value them as rituals. To us they are the ordinary — sometimes comforting, sometimes mind-deadening — activities that give a familiar sameness to our life. Far from honoring them, we pay them no heed. We see them as routines, not as paths to awareness.

My time in the monastery taught me otherwise. To be sure, the monks lived a life of deep sacramentality and prayer, and that was the true source of their spiritual vision. But the mindful practice of their spiritual exercises spilled over into the way they carried on their daily affairs. They were present to nuance, aware of the space around events. A cup of tea, a meal partaken, a moment shared with another — all commanded their absolute focus. They had tuned their spirits to a fine and subtle sensitivity, and nothing passed unnoticed or unhonored.

With the memory of the monks alive in my heart, I lift my morning cup of coffee toward the dawn. It is not a grand gesture, surely not the equal of great acts of piety or spiritual purification. But in doing so I call myself to awareness. With this simple gesture of acknowledgment, I raise this common act from routine to ritual, and invest my day with an attitude of praise.

passages

We become artists when we see with our hearts instead of our eyes.

THE GIFT OF CLOUDS

I step outside into a bracing morning. The day is almost too blue; the air is so clear that it seems alive. Far above me the clouds march in celestial cadence across the sky.

Years ago I used to drive a cab for a living. There was a blind woman I used pick up at one of the local universities. She was taciturn, proper, almost British in her sense of propriety and reserve. And though she seldom talked, we gradually became friends.

One day I asked her what one thing she would wish to see if, for only one minute, she could have the gift of sight.

She smiled and thought a moment. Then, she said, "Clouds."

The answer surprised me. Of all the choices in the wide breadth of the world, she had chosen one that would never have crossed my mind.

"Why clouds?" I asked.

"Because I can't imagine them," she said. "People have tried to explain them to me. They tell me they are like cotton. The tell me they look like fog feels. They spray whipped cream in my hand. They move my fingers over paintings of skies and let me feel the shapes of clouds painted on canvas. But I am still no closer to an understanding. Yes, it would be clouds."

I looked out the window of the cab. The clouds were moving, stately and triumphant, in majestic procession across the sky. Behind me the blind woman sat, prim and self-contained, with her cane propped next to her and her hands folded on her lap.

As I drove along I pondered her words. I, who saw clearly, spent each day wishing for some distant object — a place, a person, some prize of life I hoped to win. But one who valued sight the most — one to whom it was denied — knew that the greatest gift her eyesight could bestow was before me, unnoticed and unhallowed, at that very moment.

"Clouds," I thought. Of course. What else in this great universe so eludes description, so fills the spirit with wonder? What else floats gossamer and ethereal above our lives, never touching down but always present with us, a reminder of the majesty of an unseen God?

As a child we are alive to their magic. We lie on our backs on summer hillsides, make up stories, find giants and dragons in their forms. They are God's sketchbook, the measure of our capacity to dream.

But as we grow, they fall victim to numbing familiarity. Their poetry and majesty, though still alive in our hearts, is easily overlooked, easily ignored.

"Now, let me ask you," she was saying, "What is a cloud like?"

I returned from my reverie. The traffic was churning angrily on the rush-hour streets. Far above, the clouds were moving slowly, like horses, like carriages, like elephants holding each other's tails.

"They're like God's dreams," I said.

"Thank you," she responded.

She did not speak again. But her still, small smile filled the cab with the eloquence of peace.

*To make the acquaintance of a
tree is to gain the counsel of a
wise and compassionate friend.*

THE LAUGHING TREE

"To understand and appreciate the message of an old oak means more for a good life than all the books of man."

— Jens Jensen
American landscape architect

The birch greets me with its gentle whisper. I nod my head and pass. This is a good tree, this birch, full of the whiteness of winter and responsive to the winds.

I have never gotten to know a birch before. They always seemed too common and busy. They always hung out in crowds. I preferred the oak in its solitary majesty, or the pine in its steadfast, prayerful reaching to the sky.

But this birch is a friendly tree, most accessible, even playful. It is a puppy of a tree, alive with energy and always waiting for some small breeze to set it off in some wild movement. It brushed down against me one day when I passed, and ever since we have been friends.

I worry a bit for this tree, though. It is too easily swayed, too easily led. A bit of protection from a larger tree might calm it, give it some caution and wisdom. But it has no larger tree, only a group of like-minded birches, all too willing to join in the thrill of the chase.

I stop at the tree sometimes to see how it is doing. Is it getting too involved with its friends? Paying too little attention to its roots? Is it overextending itself, trying to do too much, go too far, before it is ready? What will happen when it is confronted with a great storm, a great darkness?

It is funny how this tree brings out something paternal in me. So many others have drawn forth the child, or the supplicant, or pointed me humbly toward the majesty of God.

But trees have their own personalities, and if we would be their friends, we must meet them on their own terms.

No matter where I live, I always try to make friends with a tree. I find them so much like us in so many ways.

They have their feet on the ground, their heads in the sky. They respond to the movements of the wind, the changes of the season. They have moods, aridities, joys. They like company.

In their scale they are perhaps our most intimate companions: their lives are understandable in years, not aeons; their size in feet, not miles. We can watch them grow, give forth their fruit, send forth their young. We can touch them without feeling alien, or as if we are violating their wildness. We sense their private courage.

And they have so much to teach. Like us, their roots are unseen, and no matter how glorious the front they put up for the world, their true strength lies in the hard work that takes place unnoticed beneath the surface.

They have good years and bad years, and yet they endure. They know how to withstand all seasons, to be patient with adversity, to store up strength for the hard times. They are nourished by the land. When the wind blows, they understand the power of the unseen, and bow their heads before it. They hold on to their children as long as they must, then let them go where they will.

And they have about them a deep compassion. They provide rest for the traveler, food for the hungry. They will even give up their own lives to provide shelter and warmth for others. They welcome weaker creatures without asserting their power.

It is a wise person who seeks the counsel of a tree. An oak will teach you about strength, a cottonwood about endurance, a willow about grace, an apple or a cherry about abundance. A pine will show you humility before God in the way it takes the shape of praise. A palm will teach you about celebration.

These are not metaphors. They are lessons from the very earth itself. For trees, with their longer lives, have their characters etched more deeply than ours. And because their roots are firm in a single piece of ground, their understanding of place is clearer and more resonant.

It is not by accident that the Buddha found enlightenment under a banyan tree; or that Jesus told us a good tree must bear good fruit; or that the Iroquois designated the wise and honest people among them as "tall pines," and gave them seats of honor at the councils. All knew that the tree, our near neighbor, reaches across the species to touch us with a clearer truth.

As I pass, my friend the birch nods its head and turns slightly. Its leaves are tinged with just the slightest hint of yellow. Autumn is coming; I wonder how it will fare.

But the birch is having none of that. It waves its arms in rhythm with the wind.

"You worry too much," it laughs. "Wait till you see the song I sing right before winter."

Ask the large questions, but seek small answers. A flower, or the space between a branch and a rock, these are enough.

THE GIFT OF
THE GARDEN

... like a grain of fire
God plants His undivided power
Buries His thought too vast for worlds
In seed and root and blade and flower ...

— Thomas Merton

My road today is alive with gardens. Some are raw,
full of weeds. Others speak of order and richness and
the fecund gifts of the earth. All are gentle reminders
of our efforts at civilization and lessons in the hum-
bler ways of life.

I have not always loved gardens. They seemed
too controlled and futile. I was blind to their beauty
and their teachings. It took a friend of mine, a Jesuit
priest, to open my heart to their beauty. He was a
deeply learned man, spoke many languages, and had

earned many advanced degrees. He had spent his life in pursuit of ultimate issues: What is God, what is the nature of good and evil, what is the meaning of life? But as he grew older, he had turned his attention to the creation of a Japanese garden.

Inside a small yard surrounded by a tall wooden fence, day by day, on hands and knees, he would lovingly pluck a leaf, bend a twig, place a stone, or trim a branch until a new and unexpected shaft of light showered down and danced its magical dance upon the earth. He now spent more time with his garden than he did with his books.

I once asked him how he had come to this.

"I still ask the large questions," he said. "But I no longer seek large answers. A flower, or the space between a branch and a rock, these are enough."

He bid me get down to where he was carefully removing a leaf from the stem of a small plant.

"Look here," he said, as the leaf released and fell softly into his hand. "This looks like nothing more than an insignificant shrub. But in fact it is a small tree, strong and full, with a rich and private life that no one knows or sees."

He pointed to a sliver of sunlight beaming down

upon its branches. "I opened this to the sun last year. See how the branch is turning to the light? This took months. But I knew that by allowing the smallest bit of light to shine upon this plant, it would slowly turn its face toward the sun."

He turned and smiled at me.

"Are any of us so different from this tree — strong, full, with a life almost unnoticed? And who among us does not grow and prosper when someone shines even the smallest bit of sunlight upon us? What more do I need to know of God and faith?"

He stood and walked slowly back into his library. "If I cannot see the face of God in a flower or a shaft of light, why should I expect to see it in ideas and books?"

I have never since ignored a garden. They are, in all their richness, the bearers of great truths. A well-placed rock is a statement of eternity. A flower in bloom is creation made whole.

Life, death, earth and sky all come together in the intimacy of a garden's space. It is a metaphor too rich to exhaust, a perfect microcosm of the universe's deepest wisdom, a constant reminder that we must accept the forces of nature if we are to survive.

At least once in the course of a day, I try to contemplate a garden. The season does not matter. The weightlessness of snow, the timelessness of rocks, the timebound mutability of plants, the fragile immediacy of flowers — somewhere within is a lesson that will touch my heart and link me, if just for a moment, with the universal rhythms that are the source of all true peace.

I reach down and touch the delicate leaf of a plant. My friend's words rise up in my heart. "Everything lives, everything dies, everything leans to the light."

If I knew only this, it would be enough.

Our spirits are harpstrings,
played upon by the winds
and the light and the passing
of the hours.

THE TURNING
OF THE DAY

One PM. Or 12:30. I cannot say exactly. But it has just happened. Like a shadow passing, we have just moved from the growing to the waning of the day.

This is not a time on the clock, but a time of the spirit. A shift in light, a change in the air. I cannot give it a name, just as I cannot name the moment when I pass from consciousness to sleep. But once, each day, this moment comes, and morning with all its promise crosses silently into afternoon, and begins the day's quiet movement toward completion.

When I was a child I would feel this change,

especially in the summer, as the days of indolent freedom waned, and the shift from morning to afternoon
somehow mirrored the change from the promise of
vacation to the inevitable acceptance of its end.

I could not understand it then. Perhaps I do not
understand it now. But I honor it, for it has a truth far
greater than my mind can contain. In some deep and
fundamental way, the spirit shifts, and different colors
come alive in our hearts.

There are many such moments in each day —
when the first pale light of afternoon cuts into the
freshness of morning, releasing the mind into the
reveries of completion; when the heavy languid dark
of late night changes to the spirit-haunted dark of
"the hour of the wolf"; when the dawn reclaims itself
from the night, and that thin crease of distant gray
illumination breaks forth into the multihued promise
of another day.

To catch these cusps of the spirit is to live our
days in holy mindfulness, and to sense, in some distant reflection, the shadow of the mind of God.

Years ago I lived by the sea. Each day I would

walk along the shore, listening to the surf, searching for the magical moment when the earth would hold its breath as the tides changed. It was like a crack in time. The earth stood still, and the rhythmic washing, the amniotic lullaby of the waves, would stop and reverse itself.

I would wait for this moment, sometimes catching it, sometimes missing it — it was so subtle, like the hitch in a baby's breath at sleep. But when I was able to be in its presence, a shiver would go through me that touched the very depths of my being.

I would mention it to others, and they would just laugh. "You can't feel the tides change," they would say. But the old timers knew. "It's there," they would say. "You've just got to learn how to listen."

We all have to learn how to listen. Our spirits are harpstrings, played upon by the winds and the light and the passing of the hours. We must learn to hear their music, and let them raise melodies in our hearts.

A Sioux mother would place her infant beneath the branches of a tree while she worked so the child could have as its constant companion and teacher the whispers of the wind in the branches.

Is there a greater wisdom than this to learn? To sit in utter stillness; to give oneself over to the whisper of the trees, the play of the light upon the surface of the water, the movement of the wind against the grasses on the land?

The yogis would have us cease all movement and listen to our breath. But is it not as worthy to sit in silence and listen to the breath of God?

The moment has passed now. The day has changed. I look to the sky, and nothing is different. But the fresh light of promise has turned to the afterglow of resolution, and my heart turns ever so slightly toward thoughts of home.

Our day is but a path we tread, a gentle walk among possibilities.

A PATH IN THE WOOD

Across the road from my home is a small stand of oak, pine, and aspen. It is the far perimeter of some farmer's land and has never been tilled or shaped. It is separated from the road by a steep bank, and is really quite undistinguished. Few people bother to climb the bank to make this wood's acquaintance.

Because so few human visitors come, the animals have taken full ownership of this small wood, working out their elemental dramas and living their unobserved lives. Squirrels, foxes, birds of all varieties — it is small animals, intent upon small actions, who call this wood home.

Today my son, Nick, and I have decided to climb the bank and explore the wood. We make our way slowly and clumsily. The ground is an undergrowth of brush and fallen branches, making this an exercise in pathfinding as much as a gentle stroll. Still, he is seven, and moves easily — more easily than I.

I push aside a bush that blocks my path. Beneath it I see a small trail curving through the underbrush. It is a path worn by constant usage, padded and shaped by the frequent passage of tiny feet. It weaves and winds among the bracken, moving perfectly to avoid all obstacles. I follow it with my eyes. Once discovered, its course is obvious. It goes beneath a fallen tree, between two stumps, across a patch of field, and up a hill.

"Nick," I call. "Come look at this."

He turns reluctantly from his place far in front of me. He is proud of his ability to move more swiftly than his father, and does not like being pulled back into the subservient status of a child.

"Come on," I say. "It's worth it."

He bounds down the hill, irritated, but curious. I pull back the bush and show him the path. He stands silently, fascinated. He is staring at a world in miniature.

"The animals who made that trail must think we're giants," he says.

"And this bush must seem like a tree," I add.

I am happy. We are sharing the kind of moment that gives a father joy. But Nick is already down on his hands and knees. "I want to see like a chipmunk sees," he tells me.

He begins to crawl along the trail, but the low-lying branches and fallen limbs claw at his face and block his path.

"You're too big," I say.

He pushes forward. "Go on ahead," he says with irritation. He wants to become one with the small animals. My presence casts a pall over his imagination.

I pick my way among the trees toward the crest of the hill as he thrashes along the ground behind me. Finally, he gives up.

"You're right," he shouts. "I'm too big."

"It's not your path," I answer.

The metaphor is too obvious, the moment of instruction too inviting. I begin forming a homily about the need to make our own path through the forest of choices in life. But a shaft of sunlight cuts over the crest of the rise, bathing the wood in cathedral light, and I find myself instead recalling the words of Ohiyesa, the great Dakotah Sioux physician and thinker:

"Whenever, in the course of our day, we might come upon a scene that is strikingly beautiful or sublime — the black thundercloud with the rainbow's glowing arching above the mountain; a white waterfall in the heart of a green gorge; a vast prairie tinged with the blood-red of sunset — we pause for an instant in the attitude of worship."

By the time Nick reaches me the sun is topping the hill, turning the grass to gold. The woods are aglow. Light filters in like memory.

I put my hand on his shoulder. The words of Ohiyesa are still alive in my heart. "This might be the closest we can get to God," I say. The trees are shimmering. Shafts of gold dance among the branches.

Nick cocks his head toward me, unsure what to make of my theological ponderings. "Ralph Waldo Emerson said that no one can look directly into the face of God and live," I continue, trying to emphasize my point.

"Who's Ralph Waldo Emerson?" he asks.

"He's a man who believed that God can be

found in nature," I answer.

"I'd rather be Ralph the Mouse," Nick says as he gets back down on hands and knees and resumes crawling along the tiny trail.

The trees chant a canticle in the wind. The sun creates mosaics on the woodland floor. Amid the crackling, I can hear Nick making mouse sounds and singing softly.

The day is a prayer. We must pray the day.

An echo is the heart reflected.

THE GIFT OF THE ECHO

We have reached the top. Nick is breathless from climbing. We stand looking out over the pond.

"Listen!" he says.

He shouts. His voice cries outward, then echoes back.

"Did you hear that?"

"Yes," I answer.

He shouts again, hears himself reflected. He is beside himself with the mystery.

I understand. Little is more haunting, more inherently mystical, than the strange and disembodied sound of an echo. In some indefinable way, it is the voice of the spirit, the sound of memory.

Nick rises up on tiptoes and shouts again.

I am brought back to a time in my life, many years ago, when I was living on the side of a rugged hill, deep in a western coastal valley. Far above my house, a hundred or so yards up a winding trail, was a place of strange power. It was a flat spot, almost a shelf of land, looking out over a canyon. It seemed to beckon like a stage, and I knew, instinctively, that for generations, maybe millennia, it must have been the site of actions of great significance. Any person wanting to profess something, or wishing make an offering, or merely wanting a place to contemplate the power of nature or the meaning of life, would have chosen that spot.

I would go there when I wanted to solve a problem, or talk to God, or worry or laugh or cry or pray. When I stood there I felt a strange kinship with people I had never seen and could hardly even imagine. Different generations, different cultures, different spiritualities reached across to each other in that space. It was like no other place I knew.

For years I wondered about the strange power of

that promontory. I assumed that it had taken on a significance because it was so presentational and open to the sky. But eventually I discovered a different source to its deep hold on the spirit.

From that shelf of land I could speak in any direction and my voice would come back to me. Even the quietest murmur would bounce off the tight valley hillsides and return as a disembodied whisper. And as my voice returned to me I would hear the joy or the sadness or the supplication that lay beneath the meaning of whatever I had spoken. Isolated from context, and suspended in space, my words became music, and every nuance of intention and meaning was revealed.

Gradually I came to look upon that echo as my teacher. To listen to that echo was to hear myself in the way that others heard me — not my thoughts and ideas, but the plainsong of my heart.

A tinge of anger, an air of sadness, a catch in my throat, a tone too shrill — all the truths I tried to hide were present in that echo. It was the mirror of my spirit.

It has been years since I lived by that hill. But the lessons of the echo remain with me. I still listen constantly for the music beneath the words of common speech. But, more than that, I try always to look upon the world and the people I meet as the echoes of my spirit. I know that if I am speaking with deceit, deceit will be echoed back to me. If I am acting with anger, the echo of that anger will return to me in the words and actions of others.

Likewise, if I find that I am constantly cheerful, full of brightness and hope, or deeply contemplative in the presence of a particular person, I know I am in the presence of a gracious spirit, and I am echoing the gift that is being given to me. It is as if the lesson of the echo contains the secret to understanding the space between us all.

As I look at Nick, I hope that he will learn the same lesson from this hilltop and this echo. He is leaning out in the direction of the small valley and cupping his hand around his mouth and shouting.

"This should be your secret place," I say. But he does not answer. He is too busy calling out nonsense syllables and the names of his cats.

I consider trying again to get his attention. But I do not. There is no need. In his echo I hear the joyful music of discovery.

We all live in a fear of being judged by others, while the empty space between us is waiting to be filled by a simple gesture of honest caring.

A NEIGHBOR
AND A FRIEND

I see her standing in her front yard, glowering. She is jabbing at a patch of offending leaves with a rake.

Myra is ornery, hard to like. Raised on the plains of North Dakota, she asks no quarter and gives none. The world as she sees it is full of fools, damn fools, and crooks. I am not sure into which category I fall. Our relationship has been an uneasy truce. Though we are neighbors, we have never become close.

"She's had a hard life. She's got a good heart," I tell myself. "Treat her with kindness." But it is not so easy. She turns every conversation to herself, berates people that I know to be gentle and generous, and shoots at our cats with buckshot.

I would dismiss her altogether if it were not for Craig, and the lesson he taught me long ago.

Craig passed through my life briefly but intensely — much the way he did everything.

He was one of those people who brought energy and life into any room he entered. He had an uncanny ability to focus his entire attention on you while you were talking, so you suddenly felt more important and more responsible than you had before he was listening. He made you better by being around him. People loved him.

One autumn day we were sitting together, half talking and half working on some now forgotten projects for our graduate degrees. I was staring out the window when I noticed one of my professors crossing the street. He had been away all summer and we had not parted on good terms. I had taken great offense at some suggestion he had made, and had in turn given great offense in my answer. We had not seen each other since that day.

"Damn it," I said to Craig. "I don't want to see him."

"Why not?" Craig asked.

"We don't get along," I said. "The guy just doesn't like me."

Craig looked down at the passing figure. "Maybe you've got it wrong," he said. "Maybe you're the one who's turning away, and you're just doing that because you're afraid. He probably thinks you don't like him, so he's not friendly. People like people who like them. It's that simple. Someone's got to break the cycle."

His words smarted. I walked hesitantly down the stairs into the parking lot. I greeted my professor warmly and asked how his summer had gone. He looked at me, genuinely surprised. He put his arm over my shoulder. We walked off together talking. Out of the corner of my eye I could see Craig at the window smiling broadly.

It was so simple, yet I had never seen it. I was coming to all my encounters with a fear that others were judging me, when in fact, they were worrying about how I would judge them. We were all living in fear of each other's judgment, while the empty space between us was waiting to be filled by a simple gesture of honest caring.

Craig understood this. He knew that all we need is to open our hearts and show a genuine concern for others and what is important in their lives.

That was what made him so special. He basked in people like basking in sunlight. Their lives warmed him and they loved sharing themselves with him.

Myra has gathered the offending leaves and dispatched them to a pile in the corner of her yard.

"Damn leaves," she says as I pass.

"A conspiracy between God and gravity," I respond.

Then I think.

"That's a pretty sweater," I say.

She snorts.

"If I didn't have a wife," I continue, "we'd go out dancing."

She snorts again. I continue on my way. But as I pass, I see her push an errant strand of hair back into place and adjust the collar on her sweater.

She looks around to make sure that no one was watching, then returns to her raking.

*Memory is a fickle thing, a
flickering light in a darkroom
of possibilities.*

THE GIFT OF THE BLUE MOMENT

I do not know who painted the pictures of my life imprinted on my memory. But whoever he is, he is an artist.

— Rabindranath Tagore

Her garden has fallen to ruin. Irene is old now, maybe ninety. Her memory has fled, leaving her eyes like lights in an empty room. I always try to say "hello" to her when I see her. She is guileless, full of wonder, a child in awe of the universe.

Her garden used to be the most beautiful around. She took such pleasure in tending its flowers and plants. She and my wife would share knowledge of bulbs and buds.

There is no such knowledge in Irene now. Her

eyes are watching other worlds. When she answers at all, it is in response to questions only she can hear.

I listen to her closely. What remains alive in the dim chambers of her memory?

She thinks I am her son, goes on about her mother. A story about a little dog. It makes no sense.

But this is not about sense. She has woven other tapestries from the threads of her life. She is responsive to other colors, moved by other winds.

I would leave, but there are echoes here.

I am carried back to a time years ago when I was living in the medieval university town of Marburg, Germany.

I was 25, penniless, alone, frightened, and ill. I was living in a garret. I had no friends and I was far from family. My days were spent working in an antique restoration shop of an embittered alcoholic man, and my nights were spent wandering the streets watching the passing lives of people who neither spoke my language nor knew of my cares.

I had never been so alone.

The mother of the man for whom I worked was a very insightful woman. As a child of twelve she had watched the Nazis come into her classroom and take the Jewish children away. No one spoke of it and class went on as if nothing had happened. But day by day, night by night, she saw her friends and play-mates disappear.

She became a watcher and a survivor.

For months she watched me struggle with the demons that were driving me. She would see me sit-ting with the neighborhood children, drawing car-toons in the shadow of the castle. She would see me staring vacantly into the distance when I thought no one was watching.

One day she took me aside.

"I watch you," she said. "I see the loneliness in your eyes. I watch your heart running away. You are like so many people. When life is hard, they try to look over the difficulty into the future. Or they long for the happiness of the past. Time is their enemy. The day they are living is their enemy. They are dead to the moment. They live only for the future or the past. But that is wrong.

"You must learn to seek the blue moment," she said.

She sat down beside me and continued. "The blue moment can happen any time or any place. It is a moment when you are truly alive to the world around you. It can be a moment of love or a moment of terror. You may not know it when it happens. It may only reveal itself in memory. But if you are patient and open your heart, the blue moment will come. My childhood classmates are dead, but I have the blue moment when we looked in each other's eyes."

I turned and stared into her lined and gentle face.

"Listen carefully to me," she continued. "This is a blue moment. I really believe it. We will never forget it. At this moment you and I are closer to each other than to any other human beings. Seize this moment. Hold it. Don't turn from it. It will pass and we will be as we were. But this is a blue moment, and the blue moments string together like pearls to make up your life. It is up to you to find them. It is up to you to make them. It is up to you to bring them alive in others."

She brushed her hand through my hair and gave me a pat on the side of the head.

"Always seek the blue moment," she said, and returned to her work.

Irene's mind is wandering now. A little dog. Her sister. Names I've never heard.

I smile and nod. She smiles back and continues. The blue moments are calling to her, filling her memories with light.

Charting a hopeful course toward our dreams is the surest way to bring those dreams to pass.

WHY BIRDS FLY

By concentrating the thoughts, one can fly.

— The Suramgama sutra

Birds are passing overhead. They are like stars in motion, music in the sky. As always, they remind me of Nikki.

Nikki was a friend of mine, and very dear to my heart. She had cerebral palsy, and to all the world she looked like one of God's cruel jokes. She could not walk unaided. Her legs were useless sticks; her arms, helpless bird wings. When she talked her head lolled and spittle dripped down her chin. Her voice was a grating and unintelligible bray.

More than once I saw parents in supermarkets

turn their children away when they saw her coming. She was a reminder of their darkest fears about life gone terribly and irretrievably wrong.

I used to love to talk to Nikki — not out of some twisted motive of self-congratulation, or because she was a dark mirror of my own good fortune, but because she was so full of life. She had a mischievous twinkle in her eye and a reservoir of joy that was deeper than anything I could imagine.

Perhaps most astonishing to me was the quality of her dreams. Her days were spent in a "sheltered workshop" sitting at a long lunchroom table putting spatulas in plastic bags with her toes. But at night she wrote — holding a notebook with one foot and the pencil between the toes of the other — creating poems, visions, stories of birds in flight.

And she wrote of love — poems to a nonexistent and unknown lover.

"Someday I'm going to get married," she told me.

I smiled and nodded. But, like the parents in the supermarket, I averted my eyes.

Gradually I lost touch with Nikki. Though she was often in my thoughts, our lives went separate ways. Then, by chance, a year later I saw her on the street in front of a store, sitting in her wheelchair.

"Kent!" she called in her clumsy and halting voice. She was flapping her arms in excitement. As I approached she jabbed her hand toward me.

"Look!"

I stared at the useless paw. On her ring finger was a gold band with a small diamond.

"See!" she said, twisting her jaw and rolling her head. "I told you."

She had met him at the workshop. He, too, had seen in her what I saw. They had courted for several months, and, himself misshapen, he had not been afraid of the limitations of her twisted and helpless body.

They planned to marry in the spring.

Sometimes, when I am engulfed in personal darkness, I see the image of Nikki's face before me. She was, for me, the embodiment of all that is confusing, mysterious, and ultimately joyful about this adventure we call life.

She could have been like so many of the others she worked with — embittered, angry, cursing the

God that made them. And none would have blamed her, for the unfairness of her life was cause enough for bitterness and despair.

But Nikki was not like the others. She would not give her heart to bitterness and despair. Instead, she set her heart on love, and in her hope she had called that love to her.

So much is made these days about the power of intention, about how we can have what we want, how we can be what we want, how our lives can be perfect, if only we have the courage to visualize our dreams.

But no amount of intention, no amount of visualization would have gotten that poor tragic body to walk. Those useless limbs, those atrophied muscles, those bent and brittle bones made mockery of any claims that right thinking and good intentions would have her rise from her chair and cross a room like you or me.

Yet, it was the power of intention that brought Nikki to love. Had she not believed in love when all about her doubted, she would not have found that love.

Nikki's true gift was to know the shape her dreams could take, and to set her course towards them. She did not dream of walking — that would have taken a lightning bolt from the hand of God. And though she might secretly have wished for that, she could not build her life around that hope. But she could, and did, dream of love, and through her faith, that dream of love had become real.

Like Nikki we must all learn to know the shape our dreams can take, and to set our course toward them.

Make no mistake about it: the world is a dark and brutal place. Children starve for no reason. Madmen kill innocent people and run away laughing.

Still, if someone like Nikki, whose body was a daily reminder of the tragedy and suffering and injustice in the world, could transcend the darkness and suffering to shape a world of dreams, and set a hopeful course toward them, who are we, the more fortunate, to do any less?

There is no virtue in celebrating limitation. Nothing great is ever accomplished by people whose first thought is about the reasons why something might fail. Nothing good is ever made by those who make their lives a dark celebration of bitterness, no matter how justified that bitterness might be.

Like Nikki, we must learn to direct our hearts to hope. Tragedy and suffering will still occur. Dreams will still remain unfulfilled. And though life, in all its richness, may not be ours to control, charting a hopeful course toward the shapes of our dreams is surely the best way to bring those dreams to pass.

Nikki knew this, and lived it in her life. As I stood there, looking at that ring glistening on her finger, I thought of the times she had told me that she would one day get married, and the way that I had looked away, almost in shame, at the hopelessness of her dreams.

Perhaps she saw some of this in my face. Perhaps it was just coincidence. But while I was thinking, she twisted her head and stared up at me. It was a look I had come to know well, for her eyes were the one part of her body she could control, and with them she could write epics and sing songs. This look said, "Come closer, I want to tell you a secret."

I bent down close to her.

"You know why birds fly?" she asked. Her voice was struggling, but her eyes had that twinkle.

"No, tell me," I said, unsure whether she was telling me something serious or passing along a joke.

She shook her head several times, as if gathering her thoughts, before whispering so softly I could barely hear, "Because they're so damn bad at walking."

She burst out laughing — that harsh and grating sound — then she turned her wheelchair and set off down the street, flapping her elbows like a bird taking flight.

I watched her wheel her way down to the corner. But just as she reached the turn, she held her hand up, and the ring caught the light of the afternoon sun. "I told you," she yelled, then waved her hand once, and then was gone.

Above me, the birds are winging southward. They, too, catch the glint of the afternoon sun. I stare at them as they pass, and wonder if perhaps the first bird flew because it dreamed of the sky.

To raise a child is an honor.
To raise a child well is a gift.

THE GLOVE

He wants to quit. "I just don't like it, Dad."

Sad words for a parent to hear. We hope to open our children to the world. We choose their activities carefully, with an eye to growth, an eye to learning. When we hear those words, we hear a closing off, a limiting of possibilities, and we are filled with doubts: "Should I force him? Don't all things require more effort than a child wants to give?"

But we must choose. Is this a thin wall of resistance that must be broken through? Or is this truly a false direction, chosen only to reflect our own ideas of what is important? The child is the father of the man, the mother of the woman. Do we do more harm than good to that man in the making, that woman in the becoming, by forcing those activities where the heart is not present?

"Okay," I say. "But keep the glove."

Nick looks at me strangely. Perhaps he was expecting a lecture on persistence, a homily on how all things worth fighting for require effort and sacrifice.

I take the glove and slide my fingers into it. This glove is the only thing in his young life that has the patina of history on it. All other objects he owns — his toys, his bike, his games — have become diminished from their first moment of use. They may have gained the easy grace of familiarity, but each, in its own way, has become less as it got older. The glove, alone, of the things he owns, has become more since it was purchased. It has been worn into meaning, not obsolescence.

I remember when he first got it. "I've got to break it in," he said. "The coach said so." There were overnight soakings with baseballs tied in the pocket, various hammerings and beatings to soften the leather. At night we would hear the telltale "thump" of a ball being thrown into the glove as he tried to make the unformed shape conform to some idea of the ball it was meant to receive. Each day, as it became less in the eyes of the world, it became more in the eyes of a child. He was making the glove his own.

I remember years ago being in the archives of a small university museum. The woman showing me around took a small dusty object off a shelf and placed it in my hand. It was unrecognizable to me — a clay bowl-like shape with a pinched spout. My guide said nothing, but merely watched as I maneuvered the object in my grasp. It moved easily, naturally, until it rested perfectly in my cupped left palm. Then I took my right thumb and forefinger and placed them on either side of the pinched spout. They fit perfectly into the indentations, as if the hollows had been made by my touch.

A shock ran through me. The hand that had created these was the same size and shape as my hand. Every mark, every indentation, was a memory of that hand. "You are touching the touch of someone five thousand years ago," my guide said.

This small pinch lamp — for that is what it was — was not less for its age and usage. It was more. It was the very essence of history, the very presence of other life. In that lamp I could feel the touch of another human being, at another time and place, across the span of miles and centuries. A new lamp — better, more efficient, more finely wrought — could never even approximate the meaning of this crude earthen bowl.

This is what I want Nick to learn from this glove. It is what I want him to understand as I hand him an old hammer that has the shine of my father's sweat on its battered handle. It is what I want him to remember as he considers discarding friends, lovers, lives, in search of something more, something greater, something closer to his dream.

"Life is not all novelty and freshness," I want to tell him. "It is old stone, old wood, old leather worn to the shape of our hands. What we have made familiar we have made our own, and it has made us who we are. We can move on, and oftentimes we should. Something better may await us. But those things we have shaped with our hands are our touch upon the world, whether it be a garden well tended, a book well used, a person well loved.

"And when we pass them on, the person who touches them will be touching us."

But these words are too heavy, too laden with meaning.

"Just keep the glove," I tell him. "It has the touch of your hand in it."

He shrugs, and takes the glove to his closet. Then he runs back into the yard, set free from the burden of parental expectations. I watch him through the window as he grabs a stick and jousts with an imaginary adversary.

Perhaps, sometime, far into some future night, he will take down that glove, slip it on his hand, and remember who he was.

Perhaps, sometime, long after he is gone, some child may pick it up and find that a baseball fits in it perfectly, and that it feels exactly right.

gatherings

We are not all called to be great.
But we are all called to reach
out our hands to our brothers
and sisters, and to care for the
earth in the time we are given.

THE GIFT OF FAMILY

It is afternoon — the time of gathering. The long
shadows of the day stretch out behind us.

I am watching the birds land on the feeder outside our window. Grackles, chickadees, songbirds,
and jays. Why have they chosen us? Despite cats,
squirrels, noise, human intrusion, they brave everything to return here. I marvel as they make their
peace with each other and share this common space.

The door behind me opens. Someone is returning. I would turn to look, but the birds are jostling for
position, and one small chickadee has caught my

attention. I want to see if she will gain entry, or if the other birds will chase her away.

"Hello," I shout.

Alex's voice answers. "Hi. I'm home."

"Have a good day?"

"Yeah. Pretty much."

It is the shorthand of people involved in separate tasks.

Water runs; a door somewhere in the house clicks shut.

The chickadee has made her way to the central pile of feed and has grabbed a sunflower seed. The others around her pay no attention as she holds it in her beak and shakes her head.

The outside door to the house opens again. Different footsteps.

"Hi, Dad."

"Hi, Nick."

"What are you doing?"

"Watching a bird."

From our private worlds we are coming together to weave our separate lives back into family. It is almost a homing instinct. Some of us will alight, and immediately leave again. Some will settle and remain for the night. But it is as if we all want to touch home for a moment — a talisman of the heart.

Some songbirds are at the feeder now. They move in a flurry, taking pieces of grain, flying off, depositing them in some unknown place, then returning.

Louise has come in the door. She smiles, gives me a peck on the cheek and goes about her business.

What a fragile vessel the family is. We choose our mates, we do not choose our parents. Our children are a gift and a mystery. How can this collection, so accidental, come together to form a union and become a family? My children have no more reason to return to me than the birds at this feeder outside our window. I have no more reason to return to my parents than those birds. Yet we cling to something common and call it family.

Nick's door shuts. From all corners of the house there are sounds of unpacking, rearranging, an ordering of the events of the day.

We are a closed-door family. There is no rancor in this; it is simply the way we live our lives — private, personal, attentive to our own needs and interests. We gather for common purposes — meals, travel, times of conversation — and we seek each other out one by one, two by two, as we feel the need. But we are a family of privacy as much as a family of community. The individual is our building block, and we honor that in each other.

I have other friends for whom the family is a central gathering event. Nothing is done by one that is not done by all. If one has something to offer, the others come to share. Each is part of the others' lives; community is the seedbed from which the individual grows. They would all be gathered together, watching the feeder as one.

The seed is gone now. The birds move aimlessly, pecking at hulls. I grab the bag of seeds and go to the feeder. The songbirds flutter upward, out of range.

There is movement in the house now. Conversation. Solo voices become duets, trios. The music in the voices is good.

Outside, all the birds are returning. They take

their turns. The songbirds flutter, alight, grab a few grains, and retreat. The jays strut and preen. The grackles swoop down with impunity, take what they will. Far in the background, perched in a small pine tree, the chickadee sits patiently.

I cast one last glance at the feeder. A grackle has seen my movement, stares at me with dark and alien eyes, then lifts off and flies away. The chickadee swoops in and takes a small grain of corn.

Nick comes out of his room carrying a piece of colored paper. "Dad, you want to see what I made?"

"Sure," I say. I can hear Louise and Alex in another room.

"Look," he says. "An alien dinosaur." The drawing is full of bright enthusiasm.

The chickadee flutters upward and disappears into the orange glow of evening. She was the last, and now she is gone. But she will be back. They will all be back. Though they have the freedom of the air, they have chosen us.

"It's a great dinosaur," I say. From the other room I hear the happy sound of laughter.

A meal is an act of quiet consecration, of holy service, made no less significant because it is so common.

A CEREMONY
OF THE ORDINARY

It is the wise person who sees near
and far as the same, does not despise
the small or value the great.
— Chuang Tzu

Her day was long. She is tired. But she has chosen to prepare a meal. If not for my wife, Louise, we would each grab such food as we could find and go our separate ways. But she will not have it this way.

"It is important for us to eat together," she says simply, and places the food before us. Though she would not put it in these words, it is an act she reveres, a ceremony of the ordinary.

We say no prayer, though perhaps we should.

But in a quiet way, the table itself is prayer enough. It draws us into a circle, the most mythic and powerful of all human shapes. We pass the food from hand to hand, the most sacramental of all common human acts. Though it remains unspoken, even unrealized, our shared meal creates a bond among us, and, for a moment, makes us one.

There is no mystery in why Jesus chose a meal to reveal his death to those he loved, why he chose a meal to commemorate his truth. This is the moment when we are most human, when we most acknowledge the fallibility of our nature — that we must take the lives of other species in order to sustain our own. And yet it is the time of common celebration when the taking of nourishment fills us with simple joy.

It is only natural to want to hallow so elemental an event. The Dakotah Sioux would often take the choicest piece of meat and cast it into the fire before beginning to eat. The Tibetans place the first food of a meal outside the door as an offering to the hungry spirits.

We have wandered so far from this sense of the

meal as holy gift. Our food comes too easily. We care less about sustenance, more about choice. We judge the meal, we do not honor it. Only the one who lifts the hand in preparation senses even dimly the sacred significance residing in the act.

Louise sets the plates on the table. The rest of us come and take our places. Food is passed from hand to hand. The affairs of the day are discussed; grievances are aired. We laugh, argue, share stories of the day. We eat happily, filled with the elemental joy that comes with taking nourishment. It is a small moment, but it is ours.

She smiles, helps Nick with his knife. In Japan, one who masters the gentle art of making tea can be declared a national treasure. I watch her hold his hand gently in hers. Should one who practices the gentle arts of making a home be revered any less?

Our lives are small, our dreams are great. We live with faith and hope in the small corners of our days.

CORNERS

I enter Nick's room. It is chaos. The floor is strewn with half-completed projects. Clothes lie in lumps and piles. The desk and bedside are an archaeology of recent snacks. I want to find him, to tell him that this will not do, that there will be no playtime, no freedom until some order is established.

Then Pat comes into my mind, and I hesitate.

Pat had been teaching kindergarten for over twenty years. So long, in fact, that she had almost become a child again herself.

Her classroom was a joyous place, full of laughter and play. To some of the more serious minded of the children, it was almost too raucous, a betrayal of the severity and silence that they were already learning as the price of survival in a world governed by adults.

But this did not deter her. There were hugs, small animals, baskets full of clothes and costumes; colors, shapes, signs that meant nothing at all. Put them on, march around, crawl on the floor. Speak in a language that no one else knows. Draw a picture of something that no one has seen.

What's your name today? Why don't we all talk backwards? What would a starfish say to a star?

And gradually they all came to her. She was a gift to behold, the wonderment of childhood writ large upon their hearts.

"What is the secret?" I asked her, as the children filed out, their minds full of kaleidoscopes and pinwheels and dinosaur dreams.

"Corners," she said. "All children need corners."

I looked around the classroom. Small piles of stones in shoeboxes. Little worlds constructed in cubicles and cubbies. Corners.

She showed me a hidden place behind a bookshelf where one boy had strung a complex web of string and yarn, and filled it with climbing plastic men.

"If I could, I would give him an attic. But this

corner is enough."

We walked to the center of the room. A circle had been taped on the floor. "This is where we meet together," she said. "It is good for them to know that we are all part of a whole. But there," she continued, pointing to the corners, the boxes, the cubbies, "is where they go to dream. Show me the corners and I will show you the child."

I look again at Nick's bedroom, at the toys strewn across the floor. It is a world disordered, random, abandoned.

But in the corner, under a table, pushed against the wall, a splash of color catches my eye. Curious, I make my way through the mess to get a closer look.

There, beneath the table, he has constructed a spaceship, a wild and fanciful winged creation of plastic parts populated with dinosaurs and tiny figures. Next to it miniature plastic monkeys climb a tower made of sticks and straws. Pieces of string and ribbon connect the tower to the ship.

Carefully, I back away, through the piles of obligations and responsibilities littering his floor. I return to the living room — the adult room — and take a seat in my chair in the center of the house.

Great joys make us love the world. Great sadnesses make us understand the world.

THE DARK GIFT

The look on her face is numb disbelief. "It can't be," she says. Then, "Why me? Why now?"

It is not a great injury — a broken ankle. But it had been so unexpected. A few hours ago she was running about, preparing for college, worrying about books and her car and which classes to choose. Now she is sitting, staring vacantly at the heavy cast on her leg, wondering why it had to happen to her.

This is the first time Alex has collided with an indifferent world. Everything else has been negotiable, has been arguable. Everything else up to now could be avoided, escaped, bought off, laughed away.

But this is real; this is hers. No one can change it, make it right, make it fair. It is life — an absolute without explanation — that is indifferent to her plans and dreams.

We try to comfort her and tell her it will be all right. Stories flow of broken bones we have experienced; jokes are told about coathangers and casts. But at heart, there is a small darkness, absolute and irrefutable, that separates us from her and leaves her ultimately and utterly alone.

"This is the dark gift," I tell her.

"Gift?" she says, almost derisively.

"Now you know."

"What do I know?" she protests. "I know that my life is ruined."

"No, your life isn't ruined. Now your life is your life. No one else can fix it or change it. No one else can be blamed. This is yours. And it is up to you what you will make of it."

She hobbles off, consumed in her own sadness. It hurt me to have sounded so callous. But this is a harsh truth, and there was no virtue in denying its existence.

The dark gift. It comes to us all. The truth you

cannot deny that makes you one with the aloneness of others.

I remember the time, years ago, when I, too, had broken an ankle. It was March; the streets were slush and the paths at corners were precarious hard-packed trails through mounds of ice and snow. I was struggling on crutches, trying to balance on uneven surfaces of ice. People were pushing past me, mutter-ing about how they had to get through, about how I was taking so long. I would try gingerly to make my way up over the snowpack without slipping or letting my cast drag in the slush. My arms ached from the tension, my shoulders were rigid and numb from the digging pain of the crutches. I tried to block out the others around me, not to feel them brushing brusquely past me.

Crutch by crutch I made my way down into the street. Cars flew by, splashing slush on my cast. I hob-bled into the street. The approaching cars were not slowing. I tried to hurry, but the icy ground was too precarious. Cars slid to a stop and drivers leaned on their horns. I was consumed with my own fragile bal-ance, ashamed of my deliberate pace, frustrated at others' lack of concern.

As I started into the street I looked across at the snowbank I would have to negotiate on the opposite side. There, making her way down through the small uneven pathway of ice, was an old woman with a cane. People were standing behind her, muttering. She was feeling with her foot, trying to find solid ground. No one could help her; there was not enough room for two abreast. I could see her frantic look, her shaking hands. Then, for an instant, she looked up. Across the distance of that icy, slush-filled street our eyes met. The fear, the sadness, the frustration, the utter aloneness of our respective plights, were mirrored in our respective gazes.

I wanted to help her, but I could not. I could barely make my way across the street on my own. The other pedestrians rushing past us both did not see. To them we were impediments to the necessary pace of daily living. To the drivers in the long line of cars that was backing up in the street, we were insufferable obstructions. We approached each other from the opposite directions. As we passed, we glanced at each other.

"Hi," I said, not knowing what else to say.

She, who had the added fear of being elderly

and alone on a city street, did not know whether to answer. Finally, she said, very softly, "Hello." Cars honked at the further slowing of pace that had been caused by our brief conversation. Other walkers brushed against us in their rush to get to the other side.

We looked again at each other, then went our ways. The cars revved up and drove past in anger as soon as we were out of their path.

When I got to the other side I turned to see how the woman was doing. She was feeling at the path in the snow with her cane. Cars were splashing slush on the back of her overcoat. She did not turn to look at me. Her solitary struggle was enough.

I want to tell Alex this story. But she is lost in her own world. She does not need anecdotes about other injuries or other people's misfortunes.

I watch her as she puts her pack on her back and moves on unsteady crutches down the hallway. She has an evening class she must attend. "I never knew that doorknobs could be so much work," she says as she balances on one leg and tries to open the door.

"Steps, revolving doors, taking baths, crossing

streets. You've got a lot of fun ahead of you," I say.

Her pack slips off her shoulder and almost pulls her over. I want to help her. But there is nothing I can do. "I'll never make fun of old people again," she says.

I smile sadly.

"It'll be a good year of learning," I say.

She closes the door and hobbles off into the street, into her life, into a night she never knew existed.

departures

*None of us is promised
tomorrow. Today, in all its
beauty, is all we have.*

THE DISTANT SHORE

For what does the Lord require of
you, but to do justice, to love kind-
ness, and to walk humbly with your
God?

— The book of Micah,
chapter 6, verse 8

Tonight word came that my friend Al drowned. He was a man of immense dignity and humility. He worked with his hands — a carpenter. I had often thought, in the silence of my own heart, that he is what Joseph, the father of Jesus, must have been like: quiet, accepting, a man of good humor, gentle rectitude, and honor.

No one knows exactly what happened. He was a strong swimmer, a man of caution, disinclined toward foolish acts. Something must have gone terribly wrong. His time, quite simply, had come.

My grief is deep, like a wound. I want to raise it up, to consecrate it. But Nick lies in his bed, awaiting my goodnight visit.

"Are you ready?" I say.

He smiles and turns toward me, makes a place next to him beneath the covers.

I lie in his bed beside him. "Have you said your 'Thank you, God'?" I ask.

He looks sheepish. Prayer, for him, as for me, is a private act. He nods, hoping that will end the issue.

I snuggle close to him and say, without ceremony, "Thank you, God, for the gift of life." It is not much, but it is enough. It is an offering I make with him, each morning, each evening. If he can take this to heart, I will be satisfied.

None of us is promised tomorrow. Today, in all its beauty and sadness and complexity, is all we have. This light we see may be the last such day we have on this earth. There is no certainty, beyond the fact that one day we will have no tomorrow, and that it is not ours to know when that day will be.

Nick falls asleep quickly. The rhythmic heaving

of his chest tells me I can rise and leave.

I walk across the room and touch a board Al once nailed in our house. It is all that is left — a touch of a touch made by his hand.

My hand lingers there. I think of him, and how he now swims toward a far land unknown to those of us who remain behind. I wish him peace, and honor his memory. There is no more I can do.

As I leave I look across at my son. He is sleeping gently. The quiet rise and fall of his breathing is like waters lapping at a distant shore.

Thank you, God, for the gift of life. Thank you, God, for the moment of light.

Our heart is known by the path we walk.

THE CLOSING
OF THE DAY

Night is closing in. It is time for sleep.

I have walked a quiet path today. I have done no great good, no great harm. I might have wished for more — some dramatic occurrence, something memorable. But there was no more. This was the day I was given, and I have tried to meet it with a humble heart.

How little it seems. We seek perfection in our days, always wanting more for ourselves and our lives, and striving for goals unattainable. We live between the vast infinities of past and future in the thin shaft of light we call "today." And yet today is never enough.

Where does it come from, this strange un-quenchable human urge for "more" that is both our blessing and our curse? It has caused us to lift our eyes to the heavens and thread together pieces of the universe until we can glimpse a shadow of the divine creation. Yet to gain this knowledge, we have sometimes lost the mystery of a cloud, the beauty of a garden, the joy of a single step.

We must learn to value the small as well as the great.

In the book of Micah, the prophet says, "And what does the Lord require of you but to do justice, to love mercy, and to walk humbly with your God?"

Confucius told his followers, "Bring peace to the old, have trust in your friends, and cherish the young."

Do we really need much more than this? To honor the dawn. To visit a garden. To talk to a friend. To contemplate a cloud. To cherish a meal. To bow our heads before the mystery of the day. Are these not enough?

The world we shape is the world we touch —

with our words, our actions, our dreams.

If we should be so lucky as to touch the lives of many, so be it. But if our lot is no more than the setting of a table, or the tending of a garden, or showing a child a path in a wood, our lives are no less worthy.

I crawl into my bed, feel the growing warmth of the covers, hear the quiet rhythms of my wife's gentle breathing.

Outside, the wind blows softly, brushing a branch from the birch against the house.

To do justice. To love mercy. To walk humbly with our God.

To bring peace to the old. To have trust in our friends. To cherish the young.

Sometimes, it seems, we ask too much. Sometimes we forget that the small graces are enough.

ACKNOWLEDGMENTS

To my friend and publisher, Marc Allen, who always looks toward the light.

To my friend and agent, Joe Durepos, who urges me to fly but always keeps me tethered.

To the people at New World Library, who make the creation of a book a family event.

To Sandy Hannum of Reading's Fun, who knows how to offer clear and cogent counsel.

To Jason Gardner, who loves the language, and treats it with uncommon care.

To my wife, Louise, whose love is my rock.

To my son, Nick, who keeps my eyes on the day.

To my stepdaughter, Alex (more "daughter" than "step") who shines light on the future.

To Jeff Wade's 5th grade students at Northern School in Bemidji, Minnesota, who have shared in the process of creating this book.

And to all the family, friends, and acquaintances who offer the small graces that make my life a blessed and endlessly fascinating passage.

To each of you I say a heartfelt "thank you."

ABOUT THE AUTHOR

Kent Nerburn holds a Ph.D. in Religion and Art. He is an accomplished sculptor with major works in such diverse settings as Westminster Benedictine Abbey in Mission, British Columbia, and the Peace Museum in Hiroshima, Japan. For several years he worked with the Ojibwe of Minnesota helping collect the memories of the tribal elders.

He is the author of the highly acclaimed books *Simple Truths*, *A Haunting Reverence*, and *Letters to My Son*, as well as the award-winning *Neither Wolf nor Dog: On Forgotten Roads with an Indian Elder*. He is editor of *Native American Wisdom*, *The Soul of an Indian*, and *The Wisdom of the Great Chiefs*.

He lives with his wife, Louise Mengelkoch, and their family in northern Minnesota.

If you would like to learn more about Ohiyesa, the Dakotah Sioux writer who is quoted in this book, read Kent Nerburn's compilation of his work, *The Soul of an Indian*.

New World Library is dedicated to
publishing books and cassettes that inspire
and challenge us to improve the quality
of our lives and our world.

Our books and cassettes are available
in bookstores everywhere.
For a catalog of our complete library
of fine books and cassettes, contact:

New World Library
14 Pamaron Way
Novato, CA 94949

Phone: (415) 884-2100
Fax: (415) 884-2199
Or call toll-free (800) 972-6657
Catalog requests: Ext. 900
Ordering: Ext. 902

E-mail: escort@nwlib.com
http://www.nwlib.com